MESSAGE

OF

GOVERNOR A. J. HAMILTON,

TO THE

TEXAS STATE CONVENTION.

DELIVERED FEBRUARY 10, 1866.

AUSTIN:
PRINTED AT THE STATE GAZETTE BOOK AND JOB OFFICE.
1866.

GOVERNOR'S MESSAGE.

EXECUTIVE OFFICE,
AUSTIN, FEB. 10, 1866.

Gentlemen of the Convention:

Having been informed, by a committee of your honorable body, of your organization and readiness to proceed to the business for which you have been convened, and to receive any communication which I may think proper to make, I feel it to be my duty to state to you, frankly, and as briefly as possible, my views upon the important subjects which will most probably engage your attention.

I received my appointment, as Provisional Governor of Texas, from the President of the United States, on the 17th day of June, Anno Domini, 1865. In his proclamation of that date, conferring the appointment, the President made it my duty, "at the earliest practicable period, to prescribe such rules and regulations as might be necessary and proper for convening a Convention, to be composed of Delegates to be chosen by that portion of the people of Texas who are loyal to the United States, and no others, for the purpose of altering or amending the Constitution thereof;" and vesting in me "authority to exercise within the limits of said State, all the powers necessary and proper to enable such loyal people of the State of Texas to restore said State to its constitutional relations to the Federal Government, &c., &c., *provided*, that in any election that may be hereafter held for choosing Delegates to any State Convention, as aforesaid, no person shall be qualified as an elector, or shall be eligible as a member of such Convention, unless he shall have previously taken and subscribed the oath of amnesty, as set forth in the President's proclamation of May 29th, 1865, and is a voter, qualified as prescribed by the Constitution and laws of the State of Texas, in force immediately before the 1st day of February, 1861."

The President's Amnesty Proclamation, of the 29th of May, made it the duty of the Secretary of State of the United States to prescribe rules and regulations for administering and recording the amnesty oath, so as to insure its benefits to the people, and guard the Government against fraud.

On the day of the issuance of the President's proclamation, Mr. Seward issued a circular from the Department of State, in which he directed that "the oath prescribed in the President's proclamation may be taken and subscribed before any commissioned officer, civil, military or naval, in the service of the United States, or any civil or military officer of a loyal State or Territory, who, by the laws thereof, may be qualified for administering oaths."

From this it will be seen that according to a strict construction of the rules prescribed by the Secretary of State, none but a commissioned officer, civil, military or naval, in the service of the United States, or a civil or military officer of a loyal State or Territory, qualified by the laws thereof, for administering oaths, could properly administer the oath of amnesty and make return thereof. If I had acted upon this rule, as prescribed by the Secretary of State, large numbers of the people of Texas would have been unable to avail themselves of the clemency of the President, and thus qualify themselves to vote for Delegates to a Convention, within any reasonable time. Owing to the immense extent of our inhabited territory, many persons would have been obliged to travel great distances to find an officer competent to administer the oath of amnesty. Under these circumstances I determined to act in the spirit, rather than in strict accordance with the letter of my instructions. I ventured upon the plan of organizing a Board, in each county in the State, so constituted as to justify the expectation of firm and impartial action, for the purpose of administering the oath of amnesty to the people, at the least possible expense and inconvenience. I knew well the beneficent purpose of the President, and his anxiety that the people should qualify themselves, as speedily as possible, to vote for Delegates to a Convention. I trusted confidently to the justice and liberality of the President to approve of a departure from instructions, for the purpose of carrying into effect his policy ; and I hoped that a measure intended to promote the interest and convenience of the people, would be appreciated, and received in a spirit of commendation instead of complaint.

I have reason to believe that some persons who are entitled to respectful consideration, are of opinion that I transcended the powers vested in me by the President, when I authorized the Boards of Registration, established in the different counties, to determine what persons were entitled, because of their loyalty to the Government of the United States, to be registered as voters ; and also when I assumed, in my proclamation of the 15th of November, last, that persons who are within any of the exceptions to the President's Amnesty Proclamation, and who have not received a special pardon, were not eligible as Delegates to this Convention.

I think it proper, therefore, that I should briefly state my views upon these points. It is contended by some, as I am informed, that the President, himself, fixed the qualifications of voters, by the proviso contained in the second paragraph of his proclamation conferring on me the appointment of Provisional Governor. I understand that proviso to be nothing more than a limitation of the power granted to me to prescribe rules and regulations for convening a Convention, composed of Delegates to be chosen by that portion of the people who are loyal to the United States. By that proviso the President placed it out of my power to prescribe rules that would permit any one to vote who had not taken the amnesty oath, and who did not possess the other qualifications prescribed for voters, by the Constitution and laws, in force in this State, immediately before the date of the ordinance of secession. The proviso was not intended to fix a rule for the benefit of the people. It was intended to fix a rule for me, in the nature of a limitation upon my powers, and for the purpose of guarding against weak and inconsiderate action on my part. In my judgment, it is a great mistake to assume that a man is to be considered loyal because he has taken the oath of amnesty. The Pressdent grants amnesty to the great body of the people, upon condition that they shall take the oath prescribed, *and thenceforward keep and maintain said oath inviolate.* He does not act upon the supposition that every man who shall take the oath will thereby become loyal. He grants amnesty to the mass of those who have been in rebellion, because to show mercy is a part of the wise, magnanimous and parental policy of the Government, of which he is the head ; and continuing promises to support and defend the Constitution and the

Union of the States, and to abide by and support the laws and proclamations which have been made during the rebellion, with reference to the emancipation of slaves, are exacted, that the clemency of the Government may not appear to be prostituted to dangerous and unworthy uses.

If it had been the intention of the President to permit all persons to vote for Delegates to a Convention, who had taken the amnesty oath, and who possessed the qualifications prescribed for voters, by the Constitution and laws, in force in 1860, he would simply have made it my duty to convene a Convention to be composed of Delegates chosen by such persons. There would, in that case, have been no propriety in laying stress upon the intent that none but loyal persons should be permitted to exercise the privilege of voting for Delegates. I am clear in my opinion that it was my duty to adopt the best means practicable to ascertain the loyal persons, to whom the privilege of voting could safely be intrusted; and that no one was entitled to exercise that privilege, who was not registered in accordance with the provisions of my proclamation of the 19th of August, last.

I am equally clear upon the other point, that those who are within any of the exceptions to the general amnesty offered by the President in his proclamation of the 29th of May, 1865, and who have not received special pardon, are not qualified to sit as members of your honorable body. I would not have so declared in my proclamation of the 15th, of November, ordering the election of Delegates, if I had not felt it to be my duty to do so.

The oath prescribed in the President's proclamation of the 29th of May of last year, is aptly called "the oath of amnesty," because it secured amnesty to all for whom it was intended. The President says: "I hereby grant to all persons who have, directly or indirectly, participated in the existing rebellion, except as hereinafter excepted, amnesty and pardon &c, &c." He afterwards specifies the classes of persons who are declared to be "excepted from the benefits of this proclamation." The amnesty oath is then intended only for those persons who are not excepted from the benefits of the proclamation. Suppose a person who is within one of the exceptions to the proclamation, to take the oath prescribed therein. What benefit results to him from taking the oath? It is not, so far as he is concerned, an oath of amnesty, for it brings no amnesty to him. For such a person to take this oath would be an idle and unmeaning ceremony, were it not that the Attorney General of the United States, in a circular issued from his office on the 7th of June of last year, gave notice, by the direction of the President, that before applications for pardon by persons belonging to the excepted classes enumerated in the President's Amnesty Proclamation of May 29th, 1865, would be considered, it must be shown that they have respectively taken and subscribed the oath (or affirmation) in said proclamation prescribed. It is only as the basis of an application to the President for pardon, that the taking of the oath prescribed in the amnesty proclamation, by any person belonging to any one of the excepted classes enumerated in that proclamation, has any significance. If a person belonging to any of the excepted classes has taken the oath, and shall not make application to the President for pardon, he has done an unmeaning thing. His condition, in the estimation of the laws of the country, is wholly unchanged.

I will not affect to be ignorant that there are some gentlemen in the Convention who are within the exceptions to the amnesty proclamation, and who have not obtained the pardon of the President. I regret that this is so. It is due to myself to say, that I have not alluded to this subject out of any want of personal respect for those gentlemen. I did what I believed to be my duty when I declared in my proclamation of the 15th of November, that such persons were not eligible as Delegates to the Convention. I allude to the subject now only for the purpose of explaining the views upon which I then acted. To pardon is the prerogative of the President. I am but his agent; and I have not felt at liberty to trench upon this high privilege. I have not enjoyed the advantage of frequent communication with the President, and I have therefore been obliged to act, for the most part, upon my own judgement respecting the duties which have been imposed upon me, and the powers with which I am invested.

I am aware that I have been censured by many persons because I did not order an election for Delegates to a Convention at an earlier day. It has been said that I ought to have caused a Convention to assemble as early as September of last year. This complaint is of a piece with that unreasoning criticism which assails every act (and especially every act of mine) which is not done in the interest, or in accordance with the views of those who precipitated the country into an unnecessary war, and brought mourning and desolation to the homes of the South. I arrived at the city of Austin in the early part of the month of August. If I had ordered an election for Delegates to a Convention to take place in the month of September, how many of the people of Texas could have been qualified to vote at such an election? Delay was unavoidable, in order to ascertain who were entitled to vote. I ordered the election as soon as I had reason to believe that a majority of the people of the State were registered as voters, and as soon as money could be provided to defray the expense of a Convention. I am, however, free to say that when I arrived in Texas, in July last, I did not believe that the public mind of the State was prepared for the immediate call of a Convention, even if such call had been, in other respects practicable. Conventions were already called in some of the Southern States, with an evident purpose to obtain representation in Congress at the beginning of its present session. I did not believe that this purpose would be accomplished; and I felt that Texas might profit by the delay to which her people would be unavoidably subjected, if the march of events, and the developements which must necessarily result from the action of other States, should be thoughtfully observed. The last few months have been fruitful of events which deserve to be weighed and considered well by all who desire to see the country restored to that tranquility which it once enjoyed, and upon which its prosperity depends.

From the impatience manifested by the press of the State at the unavoidable delay in calling a Convention, I had reason to hope that the great body of the people who had qualified themselves to vote, would participate in the election. Surely the magnitude of the interests to be committed to your charge, together with the bitter experience resulting from the action of a minority Convention in the past, were sufficient to justify the expectation that the acts of this body would carry with them, all the weight and sanction which ought of right, to belong to the conclusions of representatives, chosen by a majority of the people. I would be wanting in candor if I did not declare that the apathy manifested by the people in the recent election fills me with deep concern. From the returns made to the Department of State, and the reports that have reached me from various portions of the State, there is reason to believe that less than half of the registered voters of the State participated in the election. This fact cannot, of course, impair the power of the Convention to proceed in the discharge of the high trust committed to it, but will, perhaps, in your estimation, as it does in mine, furnish a weighty reason why the result of your deliberations should be submitted to the people, for their ratification or rejection.

To what extent it is expected by the people, or may be thought proper by you, to remodel the Constitution of the State, I do not know. No one, however, can doubt that it is expected by the President, the Congress and the people of the United States, that such changes will be made in the organic law of this State, as will make it conform, in its spirit and principles, to the actual changes that attended the progress of the late war, and followed the overthrow of the rebellion. There can be no doubt that it is expected by the country that you will embrace within the scope of your action, a clear and explicit denial, in such form as may seem to you to be proper, of the right of Texas to secede or withdraw from the Federal Union : a right assumed by an unauthorized and revolutionary body of men in 1861, sitting in this Hall: a right then invoked to justify rebellion against the free and parental government instituted by the patriot sires of '76, and justly esteemed as the best hope of freedom in the world. It cannot be thought unreasonable that the people of the United States should desire a formal and solemn recantation of a political heresy so dangerous to their peace and liberties. It may be said that no act of this, or any other body of men in this State, can destroy the right, if it exists, or settle the question in any authoritative manner : and this may be urged as a reason for declining to take action upon it. It may be well to bear in mind that the people of the United States are not looking to this body for a settlement of this question. The question was transferred by the action of the Southern people, from the tribunal of reason to the field of battle, and has been settled there by a series of events, the memory of which is likely to endure as long as the American name itself. The country now looks to this body for evidence of an acqciescence in that settlement, as it has been made, and for such further action as will bind the people of Texas, in the most solemn manner, to make that acquiescence perpetual. Too much has been predicated upon the doctrine of the right of secession—too much dared and done by the people of the South to maintain it, to justify the people of the United States in accepting silence on our part as an admission of error. They are not likely to be so credulous: and if they were disposed to be so, the utterances of some of the leading presses of the State, during the past three months, would enlighten them.

The rebellion lately maintained against the government of the United States, was declared, by those who organized it, to be for the protection of the institution of slavery, which was alleged to be in danger of extinction from the action of that government. And from the inception of the war, all thoughtful and sagacious men perceived that the main issue involved in the contest, was the overthrow of the government or the overthrow of slavery. I should be false to what I believe to be the clearest truth, if I did not say that the issue was tendered by the people of the South. The government of the United States accepted the issue. The battle has been fought: amongst the most memorable certainly in the annals of mankind. Slavery has fallen, never to rise again on this continent, unless, in the providence of God, another night shall settle upon this western world, like that which followed the downfall of the Roman power, in which both liberty and civilization shall be lost.

It is not now necessary to controvert the opinions of those who maintained that the proclamation of the President of the United States, declaring the freedom of the slaves of the South, was but a military order, which was no longer operative after the cessation of actual hostilities. The wise and benificent spirit of that proclamation, has, by the voice of the American people, assumed the form of Constitutional law. It is now the supreme law of the land that slavery, or involuntary servitude, except for crime, whereof the party shall have been duly convicted, shall not exist in any State or Territory of the Union. I doubt not that you will concur with me that this radical change in the condition of those persons in our State who were formerly in slavery, ought to be fully recognized in the Constitution, and their new condition provided for. It is, of course, not now *necessary* to incorporate in the Constitution of the State, a provision against the future existence of slavery in Texas, since by virtue of the amended Constitution of the United States, it cannot exist here. But it may nevertheless be eminently proper for you to manifest in some unmistakable manner, if not your approbation of the great act of the nation, at least your cheerful acquiescence in it.

The debt created by those who were in authority in Texas, during the rebellion, in support of the war against the government of the United States, is not, in my judgement, such an obligation upon the people of Texas as will find favor with any loyal citizen, or with the government and people of the United States. To provide for the payment of this debt would be equivalent to a justification of the purposes for which it was created. There is one thought, in this connection, which I think it proper to present. Even if the feelings of the people of Texas inclined them to provide for the payment of this debt, which I would fain believe to be far from the truth, it would not be just to impose such a burthen upon loyal citizens from other sections of the Union, which have not been in rebellion, who may come to settle amongst us, or upon emigrants from foreign countries, who may be attracted, by the advantages which present themselves, to seek homes within our borders.

I am of opinion that a failure to guard the people, by an appropriate provision, against taxation for the payment of this debt, would be unsatisfactory to them, and justly offensive to the government of the United States. It may be difficult to ascertain accurately that portion of the public debt of the State which was incurred in support of the war. I have reason to believe that more than three-fourths of the indebtedness which has accrued since the commencement of the war, was created in its support. As a means of facilitating your investigations upon this subject,I respectfully refer you to the report of Ex-Gov. E. M. Pease, and Swante Palm, Esquire, copies of which will be furnished to your honorable body.

In this connection I feel it to be my duty to remind you that land scrip to a considerable amount was purchased during the progress of the late rebellion, and paid for in the paper money issued by the government of the Confederate States. Perhaps, in some instances, these payments for land scrip were made in Treasury warrants of the State.

Payments were also made, during the rebellion, in Confederate money, for portions of the University lands, sold under a law of the State, enacted before the passage of the ordinance of secession. The Commissioner of the Land Office and the Comptroller of Public Accounts can furnish such information on these bjects as may be desired by your honorable body.

The most important questions, gentlemen, to which you will be required, by the peculiar circumstances in which we are placed, to direct your attention, grow out of the emancipation of those who were formerly in a state of bondage, and who still remain in our midst. Our former slaves are declared by the Constitution of the United States to be free. Shall we treat that declaration as a mere form of words, or shall we receive it as a living truth? Shall we repose upon the postulate that the act of emancipation is only a wrong done to us, or shall we question honestly with ourselves concerning its significance? It seems to me that the events of the past five years should abate, somewhat, our pride of opinion. We have seen a war inaugurated, for the perpetuation of slavery, result in the declaration, by the most powerful of the nations of the earth, that it shall no longer exist. Let us not deceive ourselves by the supposition that the nation will fail to make that declaration good, or to redeem, fully, the high obligations which it has assumed in this behalf, before the civilized world.

In my judgment, there could not be devised a more successful mode of procrastinating our return to our original position in the Union, than to deny to the freedmen, in our midst, those civil rights and privileges, without which, to call them free would be only "to keep the word of promise to the ear, and break it to the hope."

I cannot assume to know the individual views of the gentlemen who compose this body; but I have reason to apprehend, from what has met my eye, in the form of published circulars to the people, before whom many of you were candidates, and leading articles in many of the most influential presses of the State, that my views on this subject will not be acceptable to a majority of the members of this Convention. But I feel that the present is not a time for any true man, least of all for one placed in a highly responsible position, to dissemble his honest convictions and opinions, out of any unmanly apprehension that his views will not accord with the immature and timid judgment of those who are yet wedded to the prejudices of the past.

It is a favorite phrase of many that "this is a white man's Government," and it is declared to be the main duty of those who represent the people, at the present time, to take care that it shall continue to be so. I thank God that this is a white man's Government, and I humbly trust that the time will never come when it shall cease to be so. But if, by the declaration that this is a white man's Government, it is meant that the black man is to be excluded from its benefits, and forever wholly debarred from the exercise of political privileges under it, then I most respectfully take issue with the proposition, as matter of fact, and with the views of those by whom it is maintained. Black men do now enjoy, and have long enjoyed, the exercise of political privileges, as well as of civil rights, under the Government of the United States. The election of a President of the United States might, by possibility, be determined by the votes of black men, in the great State of New York. Is it then a matter of fact that this Government is not the Government of the black man as well as of the white? And if, in the past, black men have enjoyed civil rights, and been admitted to the exercise of political privileges under the Government of the United States, is it likely that the act of emancipation, which is regarded by a majority of the nation as a great and glorious event in the history of the human race, will not be followed, in due time, by the enlargement of the rights and privileges of the people who are declared to be enfranchised?

In my judgment, gentlemen, it is the part of wisdom to provide in the organic law of the State, that the freedmen in our midst shall enjoy civil rights, on an equality with the white population of the State. By civil rights, I mean the right to sue in the Courts of the country, and to testify under the same rules that apply to the admissibility of the testimony of white persons; to acquire and hold property, real and personal, and to be placed upon an equality with white men in respect to the punishment of crimes.

More than this, I believe it would be unwise to exclude the freedmen in our midst, from the exercise of political privileges, by making the enjoyment of these privileges to depend upon the accident of birth or color. I wish to be perfectly frank in the statement of my views, but I do not wish to be misunderstood. I do not believe that the great mass of the freedmen in our midst are qualified by their intelligence, to exercise the right of suffrage, and I do not desire to see this privilege conferred upon them. But I think that progress is the great law of mind, under every free government, and I do not believe that any policy can be enduring or permanent in this country which is based upon accidental circumstances and the "traditions of prejudice," instead of being founded upon the eternal principles of truth and justice. If we fail to take our stand now upon principle—if we fail to make political privileges depend upon rules of universal application, we will inevitably be betrayed into the error of legislating under the influence of ancient prejudices, and with a view only to the present. I think that human wisdom cannot discern what is to be the future of the African race in this country. Let us not, therefore, arrogate to ourselves the attribute of Omniscience, and assume that the freedman will never attain to that measure of intelligence which will qualify him to exercise the privilege of voting for those who are to make the laws by which he will be governed.

I would not be willing to deprive any man who is qualified under existing laws to vote, of the exercise of that privilege in the future. But I believe it would be wise to regulate the qualifications of those who are to become voters hereafter, by rules of universal application. I think it would be no difficult task to fix such qualifications for the exercise of the right of suffrage as would be satisfactory to the nation, and in no degree detrimental to the interests of the people of the State.

I feel, gentlemen, that I would be wanting in the full discharge of my duty on this occasion, if I did not warn you, and the people through you, of the evil results which may be expected to follow any system of legislation in the Southern States, intended to operate only upon the freedmen, and to keep them in a condition of necessary dependence upon their former masters, at the same time that their nominal freedom is acknowledged. Justice requires that the national government shall see to it that this now despised and degraded race shall be protected in the beneficial enjoyment of the great boon which has been accorded to them. Any system of laws, therefore, intended to deprive them of the actual fruits of liberty, will meet with resistance from the Congress of the United States. Such legislation in other States has already aroused the attention of the nation, and I feel assured that a repetition of it in Texas will but increase this jealous watchfulness. Even if such legislation could meet with toleration for the present, which is not to be expected, it would be but the beginning of another agitation which would necessarily result in the triumph of the views of the majority of the nation. We are not without experience of the fruits of such agitation. The late unhappy war was but the culmination of a protracted effort on the part of a minority of the nation to impose their views upon the majority. I sincerely hope, gentlemen, that you will thoughtfully consider what is the path of duty, and safety, and that your labors may be influential to restore peace and tranquility to the country—not a hollow and unsubstantial peace, but a peace, real and fruitful, that may redound to the permanent glory of the nation.

Not knowing, gentlemen, how far you may think proper to make alterations in the present Constitution of the State, in relation to its general civil polity, I forbear to make suggestions which I might otherwise deem proper.

I beg you, gentlemen, to accept the assurance of my high respect for you personally, and of my cordial disposition to confer with you frankly during the continuance of your labors.

A. J. HAMILTON.

www.ingramcontent.com/pod-product-compliance
Lightning Source LLC
LaVergne TN
LVHW020641110826
845149LV00004B/1305

* 9 7 8 1 4 1 8 1 9 0 4 2 2 *